Ankylosaurus

The Armored Dinosaur

Dinosaur Books For Young Readers
By
Enrique Fiesta

Mendon Cottage Books

JD-Biz Publishing

Read More Amazing Animal Books

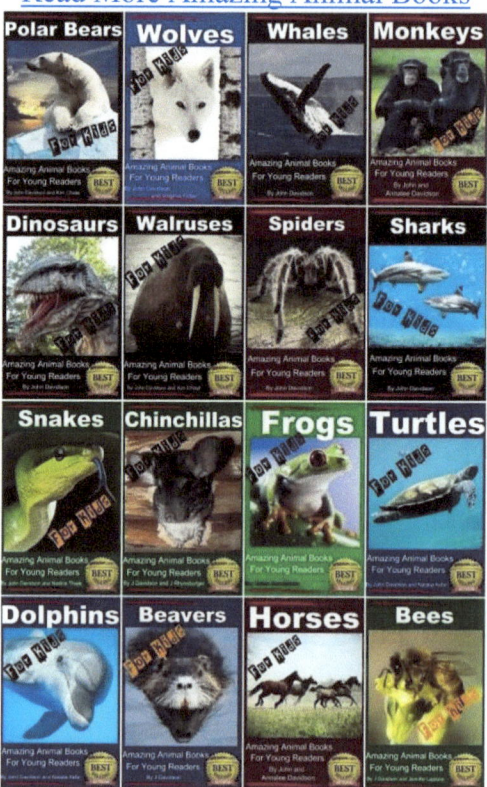

Purchase at Amazon.com

Table of Contents

Introduction

The Ankylosaurus is one of the most famous dinosaurs for a great number of reasons but mainly because of its distinctive and unique look. The purpose of this book is to go back in time to the age of the dinosaurs and explore just what exactly the Akylosaurus was, what it did, and where it lived. It is important and fun to learn about dinosaurs because they were some of the strangest and wonderful creatures to ever live on our planet. Exploring the mysteries of our planet is an engaging and worthwhile activity for people to do, and what better mysteries to learn about than the mysteries of the dinosaurs.

The dinosaurs became extinct thousands of years ago but we still have access to their bones which scientists call fossils. The scientists which study fossils are called paleontologists. Paleontologists find fossils and study them in order to learn things about dinosaurs. We are going to talk about the things that scientists have discovered and what they hypothesized dinosaurs did. A hypothesis is an educated guess. We are going to learn about the "educated guesses" of scientists. They are only guesses, no matter how educated, because it is hard to prove things about dinosaurs since they no longer exist. Even though they are guesses they are incredibly important to think about because scientists use a lot of information and connect a lot of clues in order to come up with their guesses. They compare their dinosaur discoveries to animals that are alive today; they use scientific equipment to mathematically and chemically test fossils; and they write papers to defend their arguments. The scientists take their guesses very seriously and they are passionate about exploring the nature of the wonderful and strange creatures we call dinosaurs.

We are specifically going to talk and learn about the Ankylosaurus. The Ankylosaurus is the famous armored dinosaur. The Ankylosaurus was fully covered in hard-armor, like a tank, and on the end of its tail was a club. We are going to talk about its armor, its tail, and much, much more! When talking about dinosaurs it is important that you are using your brain to think and to imagine. Imagination is really important when talking about dinosaurs since we rely on it to picture how the dinosaurs and looked and acted since we cannot see them in nature- so learning and thinking about dinosaurs is also important since it makes you use your imagination and creativity to really go back in time and "see" the dinosaurs.

It is very important to flex your imagination because the imagination is something specific to you as a human being. Imaginative vision is absolutely vital to you as a person because it is connected to how you think through problems and to how you perceive the world. The world should be a mysterious and awe-inspiring thing to you. The very fact that dinosaurs, gigantic animals in all shapes and sizes, existed should fill you with wonder (and hopefully excitement). The very fact that anything exists at all should be exciting enough! Your imagination makes boring things exciting and fills mundane things with significance if you are creative enough.

Appearance

The dinosaur we know as Ankylosaurus was discovered and named by the American paleontologist Barnum Brown in the year 1908. Barnum Brown is not only known today for discovering the Ankylosaurus, but also for discovering the most famous dinosaur of all- the Tyrannosaurus Rex. The name of the dinosaur comes from Greek. The Greek language is used by scientists for scientific names because of precedent. The Greek word "ankulos" means "curved" and the Greek word "sauros" means lizard; together the words mean "curved lizard." It is called curved lizard because there are so many curved bones fused together in the fossilized skeleton of the Ankylosaurus.

The Ankylosaurus was a very large animal compared to dinosaurs today. It could grow as big as twenty six to thirty feet long which means it could be as long as a school bus. It could even weigh up to six tons which means it could be as heavy as three cars stacked on top of each other. The dinosaur was very wide- it could be up to five feet wide at the hip. That means it was wider at the hip than today's elephants. The Ankylosaurus was quadrupedal which means it walked on all four legs. It probably had five toes on each foot, but that is just a scientific guess since the dinosaur's feet have not been discovered yet in the fossil record. The dinosaur had a posture that was pretty low to the ground which makes sense- the dinosaur was an herbivore. An herbivore is an animal that only eats plants in order to survive; because the Ankylosaurus was an herbivore it makes sense it would be low to the ground because then it could eat grass and plants without much difficulty. If you want to, you could think of the Ankylosaurus as being like a modern day cow- they both walk on four legs and they both eat grass and plants.

The most notable and obvious feature of the Ankylosaurus which separates it from the rest of the dinosaurs is its armor. The armor of this dinosaur consisted of thick knobs and plates of bone. These bone plates and thick knobs are called "scutes" or "osteoderms." The scutes were embedded throughout the dinosaurs body, so in appearance the Ankylosaurus looked like a living, breathing tank because it was covered in bone-armor. If you want to visualize what the scutes looked like you are in luck because there are animals today that have scutes. Armadillos and crocodiles are two animals today that are covered in scutes. The crocodile's back is fully armored with a thick-bone knobs which protect it from harm. It is interesting to note that crocodiles have been alive since the age of the dinosaurs- that means that the crocodile has been on the earth longer than almost every single other living animal. The armor of the Ankylosaurus did the exact same thing as a crocodile's armor: it protected the dinosaur from harm. The scutes of the Ankylosaurus ranged in sizes; they could be long and wide and cover large patches of its body or they could be small and round. The plates of armor were arranged in regular horizontal rows that ran down the dinosaur's body all the way from its head to its back. The small and round armor patches would fit in between the large plate patches. This armor is similar to a knight's armor. A knight wears solid metal pieces to cover a lot of his body, but wherever the big solid metal pieces do not cover he wears smaller metal pieces.

The Ankylosaurus also had a head covered in armor just like a knight wearing a helmet. The skull of the dinosaur was triangular and really wide with large spikes sticking out of it. The top of the skull had spikes sticking out of it while the corners of his head had spikes sticking out to the left and right. This dinosaur probably looked really intimidating, or scary, because of its armor and spiky head. What made it a really tough dinosaur, though, was its weapon; just like a knight uses a sword to fight, the Ankylosaurus used a club-like tail to protect itself from predators and other dinosaurs.

The famous tail club of the Ankylosaurus was composed of the same stuff that its armor was made of: scutes. The scutes at the end of the tail were massive and heavy. The scutes were fused to the vertebrae at the end of the dinosaur's tail. The club was very heavy and required a lot of muscle power to hold up all of the time. The dinosaur had extremely strong and extremely stiff tendons at the end of its tail which supported the club-like appendage. The stiffness of the tail also served another purpose; usually muscle tendons are flexible and elastic, but the tendons that held the club were stiff and inelastic; this means that the club-tail could be swung to deliver a strong impact because the tendons would remain stiff and would not absorb the force of the impact. Elastic or flexible muscles absorb force, so the less elastic the tail the more powerfully the tail could be swung. Scientists believe the tail was used as a weapon because of the way it looks, the heavily muscled tail, and because all other ideas seem absurd. The simplest answer is usually the correct answer. If it was used as an active defensive weapon, it could probably have generated enough force to break bones on impact. A study has shown that the large tail knobs could probably break bones. Only one other theory has been proposed as to what the club-tail was used for: it could have been a decoy head. This decoy head would have tricked predators into believing that its head was on its tail. This idea has been largely dismissed by scientists, but it is an interesting idea to consider. Some animals today use tricks like this to fool predators. Some butterflies have large spots on their wings which look like eyes. The large eye looking spots make the butterfly look like an owl face, which scares away animals that owls eat.

Environment

The Ankylosaurus lived about 66 million years ago. Humans have bee
on the earth for only about 60,000 years. This dinosaur lived during the
Cretaceous Period. The Cretaceous Period is the last of three periods in
which dinosaurs lived (Triassic, Jurassic, and Cretaceous). The
Cretaceous Period directly precedes the extinction event that wiped out
all of the dinosaurs. Scientists do not know what caused the extinction
of the dinosaurs, but whatever it was it wiped out the Ankylosaurus
along with the rest of the dinosaurs. Most Ankylosaurus skeletons have
been found in North America and all of them have been dated to the
end of the Cretaceous.

The Ankylosaurus lived primarily in subtropical regions. Subtropical
regions are warm and humid. Subtropical regions are prone to extensive
rain showers and support a wide variety of plant and animal life. The
subtropics most likely would have supported angiosperms, conifers,
ferns, and cyads during the time the Ankylosaurus was alive.

The Ankylosaurus shared its environment with a host of other dinosaurs including the Tyrannosaurus Rex, the Edmontosaurus, The Triceratops, Troodon, and several other dinosaurs. We will now briefly describe these dinosaurs and their relationship to the Ankylosaurus.

The Tyrannosaurus Rex was the apex predator of the Cretaceous Period and could grow as large as twenty feet high and forty feet long. It had six-inch teeth, walked on two legs, and probably hunted the Ankylosaurus. The Ankylosaurus, though, has strong armor and a bone-shattering mace-like tail. If a Tyrannosaur attempted to attack, the Ankylosaur could defend itself by either lowering itself to the ground to hide its soft, unarmored underbelly or swing its tail to scare away the predator. Some scientists think T-rexes could ram dinosaurs onto their sides in order to eat their prey without resistance; it is possible that that the T-rex would ramp Ankylosaurs in the side in order to knock them over before eating them.

The Edmontosaurus was a large plant-eating dinosaur that stood on two legs. The Edmontosaurus could grow as large as forty feet long and could weigh as much as 4.4 tons. The Edmontosaurus and Ankylosaurus most likely lived together without conflict since they both ate plants. The only conflicts that arise between plant-eaters is when they are competing for the same food supply. It is possible, though, that the Edmontosaurus was a browser and that the Ankylosaurus was a grazer. A browser is an herbivore which eats plants that grow up high (from trees and bushes) and a grazer is an herbivore that eats plants that grow close to the ground (like grass) which means that the two dinosaurs may not have competed for the same food.

The Triceratops was another quadrupedal herbivorous dinosaur. The Triceratops shares another feature with the Ankylosaurus: weaponry. The Ankylosaurus might have full-body armor and a tail, but the Triceratops had a huge crest lined with spikes and three dangerous horns protruding from its face. The Triceratops and the Ankylosaurus probably competed for the same food because the Triceratops was also a grazing dinosaur. Triceratops and Ankylosaurus might have grazed together in order to fend off predatory dinosaurs like the Tyrannosaurus Rex- much like zebras and wildebeest do today.

The Troodon was a small bipedal dinosaur with a large brain cavity. Scientists think this dinosaur was exceptionally intelligent compared its brethren. This dinosaur was an omnivore which means it was capable of eating just about anything including plants and meat, but its diet probably consisted mostly of small animals and insects. It is possible that Troodon ate bugs off of the Ankylosaurus like birds eat bugs off of elephants and zebras today. If this is true it would mean that the Troodon and Ankylosaur had a symbiotic relationship; this means that their relationship to one another was beneficial to both dinosaurs: the

Troodon was protected by the Ankylosaur and the Ankylosaur was kept clean and free from irritating insects by the Troodon.

Behavior

Using the information we have gathered we can imagine what kind of world the Ankylosaurus inhabited and what the dinosaur would do on any given day. The Ankylosaurus would sleep on its belly so that its only unprotected spot would be hidden from predators, but when it woke up it would lift itself off of the ground. The Ankylosaurus might have moved together in herds much like modern African herbivores-the Ankylosaurus would then move together in a herd to areas of thick grass in order to eat. If it saw Edmontosaurus or a Triceratops it would not feel threatened because they are plant-eating dinosaurs; in fact, the Ankylosaurus would probably eat in large groups of dinosaurs for protection from predators like the Tyrannosaurus Rex.

Throughout the day as the Ankylosaurus would feed large insects would home in the dinosaur to drink its blood or drink its sweat. These insects were probably very irritating and without hands the Ankylosaurus was probably unable to ward them off. Troodon would help the Ankylosaurus by running up and eating the insects off of its body.

If a Tyrannosaurus showed up the Ankylosaurus would have be careful; the T-Rex has a powerful bite and was one of the deadliest predators of the dinosaur age. The Tyrannosaur would probably try to catch the Ankylosaurus by surprise before the Ankylosaurus could get his tail ready for a swing or hide within the herd. If the herd of Ankylosaurus were able to gather together and form a circle around their young to protect them, the Tyrannosaurus would probably leave them alone. If a Tyrannosaur was persistent and continued to harass an Ankylosaurus as it fed, the Ankylosaurus would swing its tail to break the predator's bones.

In general, though, the Ankylosaurus probably spent most of its day moving around in a herd and eating grass. Predators were probably not much of a problem because the Ankylosaurus was not an easy prey to take down because of its armor and tail-club. At the end of the day the Anklyosaur would return to sleep by laying down on its belly. The young Anklyosaur would sleep close by the adults for protection.

Conclusion

We have taken a journey back to the age of the dinosaurs to learn about the wondrous and strange Ankylosaurus. We learned that the dinosaur was fully-armored like a medieval knight and carried around a club on its tail. We also learned that it could grow as long as a school bus and be as heavy as a garbage truck.

Just knowing about this dinosaur is a cool thing because the Ankylosaurus is such an interesting and awe-inspiring dinosaur. The Ankylosaurus tells us a lot about how nifty and mysterious our planet really is. The fact that the dinosaurs are so different from the animals of today should make us really think about what that means to us and to our planet.

Author Bio

Enrique Fiesta

I was born in Southwest Florida and I hold a degree in Latin and Greek language and literature. In addition to my principal studies, I have also studied philosophy, history, the natural sciences, and literature. In my spare time I devote the vast majority of my time to reading, writing, praying, and walking. I am currently pursuing legal studies in order to become an attorney.

Our books are available at
1. Amazon.com
2. Barnes and Noble
3. Itunes
4. Kobo
5. Smashwords
6. Google Play Books

Bonus Dinosaur Content

Introduction to Dinosaurs

We will start our journey with dinosaurs with the Tyrannosaurus Rex. The fossilized remains of the Tyrannosaurus are found in the world's biggest dig sites, which are located in Montana. Palaeontologists discover new things about dinosaurs in dig sites. Dinosaurs can be huge, weird, tiny and even wonderful. The Tyrannosaurus Rex, as we will find out, was one of the huge dinosaurs palaeontologists have discovered.

Tyrannosaurus Rex

The word dinosaur is derived from the ancient Greek words "deinos" and "saurus." These words translated into English mean "terrible lizard." Dinosaurs were creatures who dwelled on Earth and dominated the life of this planet during the Mesozoic Era which was about 65 million years ago. There were also flying and marine dinosaurs and they existed with the land-dwelling dinosaurs for about 150 million years. Dinosaurs occupied every kind of environment and climate which existed on Earth at those times. They could be about as small as the size of chicken to being 100 feet long and weighing 100 tons. Dinosaurs were one of two types: one was called Ornithischia which means bird hipped, and the other Saurischia which means lizard hipped. Dinosaurs could either be herbivorous, carnivorous or omnivorous. These are long extinct animals- there are no more dinosaurs today.

Microraptor© *Michael Rosskothen - Fotolia.com*

Facts about Dinosaurs

Have you ever heard of Dinosaurs? What are they? Here are some important facts about them.

1. Dinosaurs are reptiles that lived on earth over 230 million years ago.

2. The word Dinosaur originated from Greek words "terrible lizard."

3. Dinosaurs are extinct and cannot be found on earth alive right now, but their fossils can be extracted for study.

4. The heaviest dinosaurs weighed about 80 tons, and they are called brachiosaurs. Brachiosaurs had a height of 16 meters and a length of 26 meters.

5. Dinosaurs laid eggs which can be found in many shapes and sizes. The smallest egg of a dinosaur ever found on earth is about 3 centimeters in length and a large one was about 30cm in length.

6. When dinosaur eggs become fossils they harden like rocks but maintain their structure.

7. Troodon was probably the most intelligent dinosaur. Its cranial capacity was equal to that of an average present day mammal. It had grasping hands and stereoscopic vision.

8. Ornithomiminds were the fastest dinosaurs. They were able to reach maximum speeds of 60 kilometers per hour.

Fight between Euoplocephalus tutus and Troodon formosus

9. The oldest dinosaur bones are found in Madagascar and they are around 230 million years old.

10. Micropachycephalosaurus is the longest name of a dinosaur and it means tiny thick headed lizard .It was discovered in China.

11. Thecodontosaurus Antiquus was the oldest dinosaur to be discovered in Britain .It was discovered in 1970 in a place near Bristol. It was 2.1 meters in length.

12. Up to the present over 700 species of dinosaurs have been discovered and named. Palaeontologists are carrying out more research with the aim of discovering more.

13.108 species of dinosaurs have been discovered in Britain alone.

14. Megalosaurus was the first dinosaur to be formerly named. It was named in 1824.

Dinosaur Extinction

The term extinction is used in biology to refer to the end of a species. Dinosaurs became extinct 65 million years ago at the end of the Cretaceous period. Since this took place many years ago, it is hard for scientists to find the reason that caused the dinosaurs to become extinct. Rocks and fossils are used by scientists to find out what caused the dinosaur extinction. However, there are some plausible explanations for what could have happened.

The explanations put forward include:

Volcanic eruptions
Volcanic eruption are one of the suggested reasons. According to this suggestion, there was a lot of volcanic activity that caused changes in the weather. The dinosaurs were not able to adapt to the weather changes and so they died.

Diseases
Diseases could also have caused the death of the dinosaurs. A disease could have spread rapidly and killed them.

The Ice age
The climate of the planet occasionally becomes colder. These cold-periods are called ice ages and they might have killed off the dinosaurs if they could not survive in the colder weather.

Asteroid impact

Scientists believe that a very big asteroid hit the earth during the age of the dinosaurs. An asteroid impact could have altered weather patterns and possibly lowered the temperature of the planet. This is because an asteroid impact would have ejected tons of dust particles into the sky which would have blocked sunlight. If the sun is blocked plants cannot survive, then herbivores cannot survive, and then carnivores cannot survive.

Combined reasons or Gradual extinction
It is possible that no one factor alone was responsible for the death of the dinosaurs, but possibly a combination of volcanic eruptions, asteroid collisions, and outbreak of disease.

Dinosaur Fossils

Dinosaurs are animals that existed thousands of years ago. They are of different sizes and colors. Some have wings and other appear in their own physical appearance. Dinosaur fossils have been found all over the world.

Dinosaur Fossil

Fossils are what is left of these great animals. The bones that they left behind have been turned into rock over time. Today scientists can study these great animals by finding the fossils they left behind.

Dinosaur Eggs

Dinosaur eggs have been found all over the world. Some of them are very similar to large ostrich eggs found today. They have been fossilized over time and that is why we can still find them today. They generally tend to have more symmetry and a rounder shape than modern bird eggs. Baby dinosaurs found in fossilized eggs can be studied to learn more about the nature of these wonderful animals.

Dinosaur Egg

Dinosaur Names

The following are common dinosaur names and their meanings. Most names are coined from Greek vocabulary, but some dinosaurs are named after their place where they were discovered.

1. Albertosaurus -"Lizard of Alberta" refers to the fact that it was discovered in
Alberta.

2. Allosaurus -"Strange Lizard" due to its unusual bone structures.

3. Apatosaurus-"Deceptive Lizard" because it had bones similar to another dinosaur's bones. The confusion caused by this fact made the discoverer call the dinosaur deceptive.

4. Baryonyx -"Heavy Claw" because the first fossil to be found was a claw, and because this dinosaur's hands have large claws.

5. Brontosaurus- "Thunder Beast"

6. Coelophysis -"Hollow form"

7. Cynognathus -"Dog jawed" , because it has a jaw like a dog.

8. Deinonychus -"Terrible claw", refers to the large claws on its feet.

9. Dilophosaurus -"Two-crested lizard" because of the protuberances on its head.

10. Dimetrodon -"Two size of teeth" because it has a set of large teeth and a set of small teeth.

11. Dimorphodon- "Two types of teeth" possessed two different types of teeth, which is noteworthy for a reptile.

12. Diplocaulus- "Double stalk."

13. Diplodocus -"Double beamed lizard."

14. Dolichorhynchops -"Long-nosed snout."

15. Dromaesaurus -"Running lizard."

16. Elasmosaurus -"Thin plated lizard."

17. Gallimimus -"Bird mimic" because this dinosaur looks like a bird.

18. Giganotosaurus-"Giant lizard of south" refers to the gigantic size of this dinosaur.

19. Hesperonis- "Regal western bird."

20. Ichthyosaurus -"Fish lizard" because this dinosaur lived in the ocean.

21. Iguanodon -"Iguana tooth" the tooth of this dinosaur resembled that of an iguana.

22. Kronosaurus- "Titan lizard" refers to this dinosaur's large size.

23. Liopleurodon -"Smooth-sided teeth."

24. Maiasaurus -"Good mother lizard."

25. Megalodon -"Big-toothed shark" because this shark has enormous teeth.

26. Mosasaurus- "Meuse lizard."

27. Nothosaurus - "False lizard."

28. Ornitholestes-"Bird robber."

29. Ornithomimus-"Bird mimic" because of its bird-like appearance.

30. Oviraptor- "Egg thief" because they were believed to be taking eggs of other animals.

31. Plesiosaurs -"Close to lizard."

32. Pliosaurs -"More lizards."

33. Protoceratops-"First horn face" because of its single horn.

34. Pteradactyl- "Winged-fingered lizard" because of its long fingers which seemed to form a wing.

35. Pteranodon -"Winged, without teeth" because this dinosaur has a toothless beak and wings.

36. Quetzacoatlus- was named after the Aztec god Quetzalcoatl.

37. Saltopus -"Jumping Foot", because the first fossil found of this dinosaur was a leaping foot.

38. Spinosaurus- "Thorn lizard" because of the paddle-like spines protruding from its back.

39. Stegosaurus- "Roofed lizard" because it had bones on the back.

40. Suchomimus -"Crocodile mimic" because it looks like a crocodile in appearance.

41. Triceratops -"Three-horned face" refers to the three horns protruding from this dinosaurs head.

42. Trilobites- "Three lobes" refers to the tripartite structure of this creature's body.

43. Troodon- "Wounding tooth" refers to the dinosaur's sharp teeth.

44. Tyrannosaurus Rex -"Tyrant lizard" because this dinosaur is terrible to behold.

45. Utahraptor- "Robber from Utah", this dinosaur was named after the
place it was first discovered.

46. Velociraptor- "Speedy robber."

47. Yangchuanosaurus -"Yanchuan Lizard" because it was discovered in Yangchua.

Dinosaur Diet

The diet of an average dinosaur consisted either of plants, meat, insects, or some combination of the above. The dinosaurs which ate plants exclusively are called herbivores which literally means "plant eater." These dinosaurs ate fruit, leaves, grass, and roots from the earth and from trees. These dinosaurs possessed blunt, interlocking teeth which allowed them to easily grind up their vegetable diet. Some of these dinosaurs would eat rocks to help them digest their meals. It is speculated that these dinosaurs ate a lot, drank a lot, and slept a lot.

Other dinosaurs were carnivores which literally means "meat eater." These dinosaurs are more famous than herbivores because they are commonly depicted as the antagonists in dinosaur movies: think Tyrannosaurus Rex. Carnivores would hunt other dinosaurs down and eat them in order to feet. If they were anything like modern day predators, their primary source of food was herbivorous dinosaurs. Carnivores were built for speed and possessed sharp teeth and sharp talons. They would use their speed to catch their prey, their claws to grip the grey, and their teeth to kill their prey. Some of these predators lived in packs and they would hunt together in order to bring down large prey they would otherwise not be able to kill.

Omnivores were dinosaurs which ate meat, insects, and vegetation. Omnivore literally means "all-eater." These dinosaurs would generally eat whatever was commonly available and sometimes they were scavengers. Scavengers eat the remains of animals which were killed by carnivores. These dinosaurs were specially adapted because they could survive in environments where other dinosaurs would die. If an area lacked meat or vegetation, an omnivore would survive but a herbivore or carnivore would die because of lack of food.

Feathered Dinosaurs

Shandong Tianyu Museum's discovery of partial pieces of fossils suggest that certain dinosaurs had feathers. A small skeleton of a dinosaur discovered later proved that the museum was correct. The fossil possessed feathers. Now scientists are speculating that a large variety of dinosaurs possessed feathers and these discoveries back up scientist's claims that some dinosaurs evolved into modern-day birds. Many of these feathered fossils are being discovered in China. These feathered dinosaurs possessed very complex and unique teeth. They were pointed, sharp, and peculiarly large. The teeth in their back jaws were broad and flat. Their teeth seem to indicate that they were able to eat both meat and vegetation, thus making them omnivores.

Plant Eating Dinosaurs

Herbivorous dinosaurs were well adapted to eating plants because of their teeth and long neck. Their teeth were built specially for grinding down plant matter, and some dinosaurs had long necks which allowed them to eat from the tops of trees. The following dinosaurs are common herbivorous dinosaurs.

1. Sauropodomorphs

They are also known as prosauropods. They consist of dinosaurs such as Plateosaurus ,Massopondylus, Lufengosaurus and Anchisaurus. They were able to feed on trees up to a height of 1.2 meters. They had well adapted teeth which were roughened and diamond shaped which allowed for easy tearing of vegetation. They had thick muscles at the gizzards that helped to break down the food.

2. Ornithischains

They had horny peak that was sharp and protruding out of the mouth for cropping plants. Teeth were adapted for tearing the picked plant food before swallowing. They had a fleshy cheek which covered parts of the side of their mouths. In this group there were dinosaurs such as lesothosaurus, Orodromes and the Scelosaurus.

3. Larger ornithopods

They included dinosaurs such as Ouranosaurus, Iguanodonand, Hadrosaurus. They had a beak which was sharp and broad for picking plant foods. They had interlocking teeth which allowed them to tear vegetation easily.

4. Larger ceratopians

They had extremely narrow beak which resembles that of a parrot. The beak was used to feed on vegetation by cutting the vegetation. They had more than one hundred teeth behind the beak; the teeth were interlocking for easy chewing of the plants picked. Psittacosaurus was a ceratopian.

The Weirdest Dinosaurs

Let's discuss a few of the weirdest dinosaurs known to humans.

Oviraptor- This dinosaur looked very similar to a modern day ostrich.
Oviraptor was weird in the sense that it already had bird like features before it became extinct.

Ouranosaurs- They had spines coming out of their backbone which means it had a sail on its back, or a large hump of flesh like a modern day camel. Since it was discovered in a desert, it is possible that it was a camel-like dinosaur.

Carnotaurus- Looked like a tiny Tyrannosaurs Rex. The Carnotaur had horns on its eyebrows and incredibly tiny arms.

Mamenchisaurus was herbivore but what made it weird was the length of its neck. It had an enormous 35-40 foot neck and not
surprisingly, it could never stretch it to full length upwards but had to carry it parallel to the ground.

The Deadliest Dinosaurs

Here are some of the deadliest dinosaurs. These dinosaurs were the lions, tigers, and bears of their time, only much, much larger.

1.Tyrannosaurus Rex
It had numerous strong and sharp teeth. This dinosaur was incredibly large and was probably the apex predator wherever it lived.

2. Utahraptor dinosaur
It had single curved claws which looked like a knife attached to its feet. These dinosaurs might have hunted in packs which made bringing down prey an easier task.

3 Jeholopterus
This dinosaur had sharp fangs. It is believed that the Jeholopterus made a living by sucking blood from other dinosaurs such as large sauropods (long-neck dinosaurs).

4. Kronosaurus
This is believed to have been bigger than the present great white shark. It possessed bigger teeth and a bigger jaw size. Think of a whale-sized shark coming after you.

5. Allosaurus
The Allosaurus was a fierce predator. This is proven by its very powerful jaws and sharp claws.

6. Sarcosuchus

This was the largest crocodile of the dinosaur age. Its length was double that of the largest crocodiles today and its weight was equal to 10 modern-day crocodiles. It had a long and powerful neck which allowed it to jump out of the water with lightning-quick speed.

7. Giganotosaurus

It had a weight of about 8 tons and three strong fingers on each of its hands. It was the largest predator that ever existed on earth. A full grown Gigantosaurus was probably able to bring down full-grown sauropods (long-neck dinosaurs).

Flying Dinosaurs

There are several species of dinosaurs which could fly or glide. Here are four of the flying dinosaurs that inhabited the earth millions of years ago.

Dimorphodon is one of the flying dinosaurs that existed during the age of reptiles. This type of dinosaur had two kinds of teeth and it was around 3.3 feet in length with a wing span of 4 feet. Due to its inability to stand and walk, this dinosaur spent a lot of time perched when not flying.

Dimorphodon

Rhamphorhynchus in another flying dinosaur that had short legs, a long tail that was made of ligaments, and a wing span of 3 feet in length. It had a narrow jaw with very sharp teeth and had a beak which it probably used to catch fish.

Rhamphorhynchus

The *Quetzalcoatlus* was discovered in North America and it is known to be one of the largest flying reptiles during the time dinosaurs were living on earth. Its wing span was 36 feet in length, and it had large eyes, a crested head, a very thin beak and its weight is speculated to have been around 300 pounds. The bones of this flying dinosaur were hollow which meant it could fly for very long distances.

Quetzalcoatlus

The *Pterodactyus* lived near water and its diet consisted of fish and other kinds of small animals. Its wing span was 20 to 30 inches.

Kinds of Dinosaurs

There were many different types of dinosaurs. Here is how scientists have classified them.

Dino Basics
A famous British scientist named Harry Seeley, in 1800's proposed a classification based on their hip structure. Seeley classified two major groups called Ornithischia (bird-hipped) and Saurischia (lizard-hipped). These two types were further broken down into sub groups as follows:

Ornithischia
Thyreophora: Also known as the armored dinosaurs, these dinosaurs were herbivores (plant eaters) and lived in the early Jurassic to the late Creaceous age. Thyrephora simply means "shield bearers" because these type of dinosaurs had armor, plates and horns. This group included Stegosaurus, Ankylosaurusand Nodosauus.

Ornithischia

Cerapods: These are typically horned or duck-billed dinosaurs Just like the Thyreophora, Cerapods were herbivores however, these dinosaurs has better teeth that helped them grind plants better. Cerapods were able to extract more nutrients from their food because of their more advanced jaws.

Saurischia
Theropods: The name means "beast feet." Typically, these dinosaurs moved on two legs and were carnivores (meat eaters). Some of these kinds of dinosaurs were also omnivores (ate both plants and meat). Theropods lived from the late Triassic period until the end of Cretaceous period. Scientists have also discovered that birds are the evolved-descendants of Theropods. While the scary looking and most popular ones in this category are the Tyrannosaurus Rex and Veliociraptor, there were also other dinosaurs like Spinosaurus, Deinonychus, Allosaurus, Carnotaurus,

Albertosaurus, Megalosaurus, Yangchuanosaurus and much more.

Sauropods: These lizard-footed type of dinosaurs walked on four legs and were enormous in size. They had long necks and tails, were huge in size and had comparatively small heads. Sauropods were herbivores and included Brachiosaurus, Diplodocus, Seismosaurus, Giraffatitan, and Apatosaurus.

The Biggest Dinosaurs

During the Jurassic period there were many heavy, gigantic dinosaurs that roamed all throughout the earth. Some of the biggest dinosaurs are listed below:

Liopleurodon - Liopleurodon looked similar to an orca and a shark, and it was the biggest pliosaur. It had a massive body, huge flippers, and a long thick jaw full of teeth. Palaeontologists say that this type of dinosaur weighed over 30 tons and could grow to a length of 50 feet.

Quetzalcoatlus - This type of dinosaur was also huge in size as it had a wingspan of 45 feet. This huge pterosaur has received its name from the winged Aztec god.

Spinosaurus - Spinosaurus was heavier than Tyrannosaurus Rex and it is believed that they were bigger in size too. It had a mouth that was similar to crocodile's mouth and it also had a skin flap that protruded from its back which resembled a sail. It is believed that the sail helped the dinosaur regulate its body temperature.

Argentinosaurus - As the name suggests, the fossils of this dinosaur was found in Argentina. It was among the biggest dinosaurs with weight of over 100 tons and height of up to 120 feet. A single spinal vertebra is four feet in diameter.

Argentinosaurus

The Smallest Dinosaurs

Fossils have helped palaeontologists discover the smallest dinosaurs that lived on earth. They are as follows: The Humming Bird - It may seem strange, but palaeontologists believe that dinosaurs did not become extinct completely but underwent evolution. Humming birds are believed to be the evolutionary descendants of dinosaurs that lived millions of years ago. It weighs as little as one-tenth of an ounce, and is considered to be the smallest dinosaur species that lives today.

Lariosaurus - With a total weight of about 20 pounds and a length of 2 feet, this dinosaur was the smallest aquatic dinosaur. It had a long pointed tail and a streamlined body. It usually lived in water but it also dwelt on land. It was similar to amphibians because it could live in both environments.

Pterosaurus - Pterosaurus had hollow bones and were lightly built. The pterosaurs were of different sizes but the smallest one was just a few inches long. This carnivorous dinosaur ate insects, crabs and fishes.

Microceratops - The microceratops was the smallest herbivorous dinosaur. It weighed 4 pounds and had a height of about a foot and a half.

Microaptor - The microaptors were the smallest carnivorous dinosaurs. They had a height of just 2 feet from head to tail. They were also known as "four-winged dinosaur" because they had feathers on their legs and arms. Their diet consisted only of insects.

Author Bio

Enrique Fiesta

I was born in Southwest Florida and I hold a degree in Latin and Greek language and literature. In addition to my principal studies, I have also studied philosophy, history, the natural sciences, and literature. In my spare time I devote the vast majority of my time to reading, writing, praying, and walking. I am currently pursuing legal studies in order to become an attorney. After I earn my law degree I intend to pursue a doctorate in philosophy, literature, and politics.

Our books are available at
1. Amazon.com
2. Barnes and Noble
3. Itunes
4. Kobo
5. Smashwords
6. Google Play Books

Publisher

JD-Biz Corp

P O Box 374

Mendon, Utah 84325

http://www.jd-biz.com/

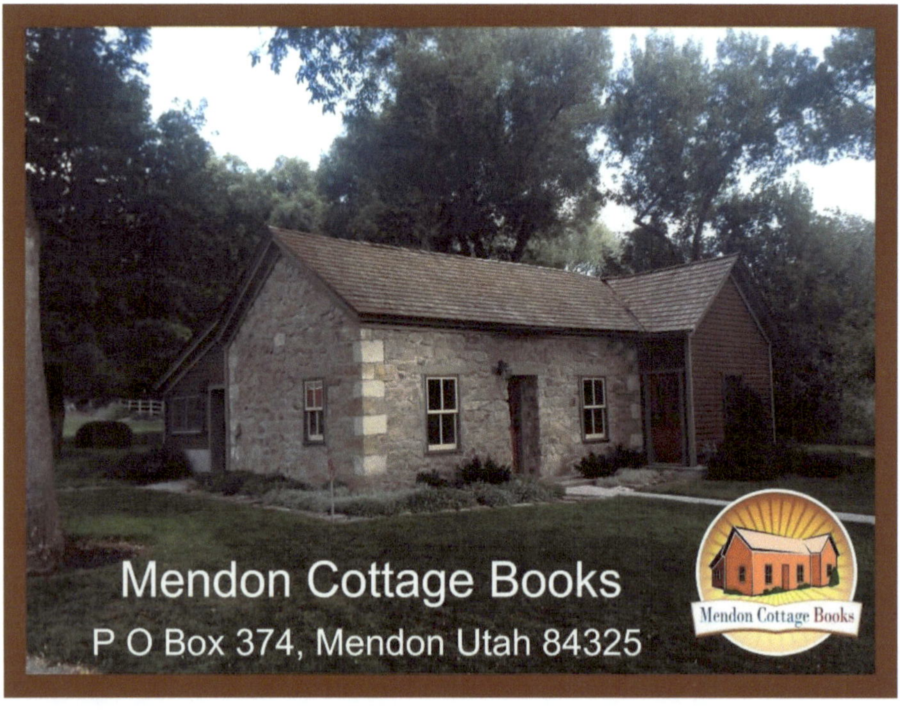

Mendon Cottage Books

P O Box 374, Mendon Utah 84325

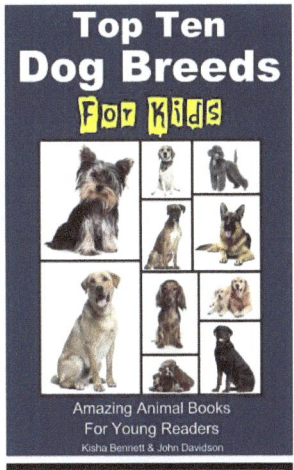

Top Ten Dog Breeds For Kids

Amazing Animal Books For Young Readers

Kisha Bennett & John Davidson

Poodles

Dog Books for Kids

K. Bennett

Labrador Retrievers

Dog Books for Kids

K. Bennett

German Shepherds

Dog Books for Kids

K. Bennett

Rottweilers

Dog Books for Kids

K. Bennett

Boxers

Dog Books for Kids

K. Bennett

Golden Retrievers

Beagles

Yorkies

Dog Books for Kids

K. Bennett

Dog Books for Kids

K. Bennett

Dog Books for Kids

K. Bennett